INTERVIEW QUESTIONS

&

ANSWERS

Sample Responses to Situational Interview Questions and Inquiries About the Company and Role in a Job Interview

STARLIGHT

STARLIGHT INYAMA

1

DEDICATION

This work is dedicated to God Almighty, for His mercies and goodness.

Table of content

Situational Interview Questions and Sample Answers

A situational interview is a type of job interview where candidates are asked to respond to hypothetical or real-life scenarios. The objective is to evaluate the applicants' potential responses to certain scenarios that could arise at work. Employers assess a candidate's ability to solve problems, make decisions, and deal with issues at work via situational interviews.

In a situational interview, candidates are presented with a scenario and asked to describe how they would respond or act in that particular situation. These situations often relate to the obligations and tasks of the position they are seeking. The interviewer wants to know how the applicant thinks, how analytical they are, and how they apply what they've learned and experienced to real-world scenarios.

A candidate may be asked, "How would you handle a situation where a team member is consistently not meeting performance expectations?" in a situational interview for a managerial position, for instance. The candidate is then expected to provide a thorough and organized response, outlining the steps they would take to address the issue.

To prepare for a situational interview, consider typical work environments and craft intelligent answers that highlight your experience and problem-solving skills. Implementing the STAR technique (which stands for Situation, Task, Action, and Result) can aid in efficiently organizing your answers.

Certainly, here are some situational interview questions along with sample answers. The purpose of these questions is to gauge your response to various circumstances in a professional setting:

1. Give an example of a time when you had to fulfill a deadline.

Sample Response: I worked on a project with a tight deadline in my prior position. I effectively managed the team, established specific goals, and, with perseverance, we completed the task by the deadline with excellent outcomes.

2. How do you respond to unforeseen modifications to the objectives or needs of a project?

Sample Response: To guarantee project success, I promptly reevaluate goals, discuss changes with the team, and make the appropriate modifications.

3. Could you provide an instance of a moment when you had to deal with a challenging team member or coworker?

Sample Response: I worked with a difficult team member on a prior assignment. I listened to their viewpoint, opened up dialogue, and we were able to find common ground, which led to a successful project.

4. Tell about a time when you had to assume leadership in a group endeavor.

Sample Response: I took the initiative during a difficult project by establishing precise objectives, assigning responsibilities, and offering assistance. This led to the project's successful completion ahead of time.

5. When you have many deadlines that are in conflict, how do you prioritize tasks?

Sample Response: To keep organized and make sure important things are completed on time, I prioritize projects based on deadlines and significance. I often use to-do lists and time management applications.

6. When was the last time you had to mediate a dispute between teammates?

Sample Response: In my past position, there was a dispute among team members on project priorities. I led a conversation and assisted the group in setting priorities, which improved productivity.

7. Give an example of a time you had to deal with a disgruntled customer or client.

Sample Response: I once dealt with a customer who was unhappy and worried about the status of a project. I kept their confidence and satisfaction by attentively listening to them, attending to their issues, and offering answers.

8. How do you efficiently manage your time while handling many activities or projects at once?

Sample Response: To make sure I allot enough time to each project, I employ time management strategies like the Pomodoro method, task segmentation into concentrated periods, and project management software.

9. Could you provide an instance of a moment when you had to make a challenging choice at work?

Sample Response: In a project with a limited budget, I had to make a difficult decision about resource reallocation. After weighing my alternatives and studying the facts, I made the choice that eventually made the project successful.

10. Give an example of a time you successfully implemented a new system or procedure to increase productivity.

Sample Response: By introducing a new project management technology, I was able to boost project efficiency by 20% by streamlining team communication and task tracking.

11. When you lack the knowledge necessary to make a choice, how do you respond?

Sample Response: Rather than making a snap choice in these circumstances, I do my homework, consult with experts, and collect as much pertinent information as I can.

12. Can you think of a situation when you had to oversee a lot of work and make sure everything was done correctly?

Sample Response: In my prior position, there was a time when I worked a lot. I made sure all jobs were finished precisely and on time by setting priorities, assigning work as needed, and staying focused.

13. Give an example of a time you were able to inspire your group to accomplish a difficult task.

Sample Answer: To get our team to finish the project successfully under a tight deadline, I inspired everyone by highlighting its significance, breaking it down into manageable steps, and offering constant support and encouragement.

14. How do you respond to circumstances in which coworkers or team members oppose change?

Sample Response: To make team members feel appreciated and heard, I actively include them in decision-making, communicate clearly, and explain the reasoning for the change.

15. Could you provide an example of a situation in which you had to solve a technological glitch or problem?

Sample Response: I ran into a technical problem with our website when working in a prior position. Working with the IT team, I carried out a methodical investigation and fixed the problem with the least amount of disruption.

16. Describe a scenario in which you had to give a teammate or coworker constructive criticism.

Sample Response: I've had to critique a colleague's presentation abilities before. I used a diplomatic approach, pointing out their strong points and making specific recommendations for development, which they accepted and implemented.

17. When you have to bargain with customers or stakeholders to get to a win-win arrangement, how do you manage the situation?

Sample Response: My main priorities are finding win-win solutions, creating shared objectives, and engaging in active listening. Recently, I was able to secure a contract extension by providing more value to our services and attending to customer concerns.

18. Can you think of a moment when you had to deal with an urgent emergency or crisis at work?

Sample Response: I ensured minimum interruption to operations during a system outage by remaining composed, initiating the incident response procedure, collaborating with the technical team, and informing stakeholders.

19. Give an example of a time when you had to assign work wisely to make sure the project was completed.

Sample Response: During a big project, I assigned responsibilities according to team members' abilities and talents, kept the team members updated on our progress, and made sure everyone had the tools they needed to do their jobs. All of these actions led to a successful project conclusion.

20. How do you respond when team members push back or show resistance when working on a project?

Sample Response: To combat opposition, I promote an inclusive and transparent team atmosphere, welcome criticism, and make an effort to comprehend issues. I was able to get the team's support for a recent project by listening to their worries and coming up with workable answers.

21. Could you provide an example of a situation in which you had to professionally and discreetly handle sensitive information?

Sample Response: In a former position, I had access to confidential financial information. I made sure everything was secure by closely following data protection guidelines and only disclosing information to those who needed it.

22. Give an example of a scenario in which you had to settle a dispute among colleagues.

An example response might be: Two team members disagreed over how to divide up the resources. To mediate, I actively listened to all sides, found areas of agreement, and assisted them in coming to a decision that pleased them both.

23. What is your approach to accepting constructive criticism or comments from superiors?

Sample Response: I see criticism as a chance to improve. I pay close attention, seek explanations where necessary, and create doable strategies to fix any areas that might need improvement.

24. When was the last time you had to work with a cross-functional team to accomplish a shared objective?

Sample Response: I was engaged in a project that was handled by many departments. By planning frequent meetings, establishing precise goals, and making sure that each person's efforts were acknowledged, I promoted teamwork and helped the project turn out well.

25. Give an example of a time you had to assume more responsibility because a team member was absent or there were unforeseen events.

Sample Response: During a critical project period, a team member suddenly missed work. I took charge, divided up the work, and made sure the project moved forward without hiccups and that we met our deadlines.

26. How do you respond to circumstances when you have to provide a subordinate with unfavorable criticism or an assessment?

Sample Response: I take a positive approach, highlighting certain areas that need work and providing assistance in learning new abilities. Team members have benefited from this strategy and have grown in their positions.

27. Could you provide an instance of managing a project under tight financial or resource constraints?

Sample Response: In a project with limited resources, I carefully tracked expenses, made the best use of my resources, and identified economical alternatives without sacrificing project quality.

28. Give an example of a time you had to deal with an unhappy internal customer or stakeholder.

Sample Response: I once dealt with an internal customer who wasn't satisfied with how the project was going. I worked with the team to resolve problems, listened intently to their worries, and kept them informed throughout, which eventually made them happy again.

29. When you need to implement a new policy or procedure for your team or department, how do you manage the situation?

Sample Response: To guarantee a seamless transition, I introduce new policies or processes by communicating with them, highlighting their advantages, and offering assistance and training.

30. When was the last time you had to deliver a complicated concept or proposal to stakeholders or senior management?

Sample Response: By dissecting a complicated idea into manageable chunks, presenting convincing evidence, and addressing any possible objections, I was able to convince top management to accept it.

31. Give an example of a scenario in which you had to manage conflicting demands from several teams or departments.

Sample Response: To ensure that everyone's demands were satisfied without sacrificing the overall goals, I collaborated with department heads, matched objectives, and negotiated timetables to handle conflicting priorities.

32. How do you respond to circumstances in which you must exercise leadership in the face of ambiguity or uncertainty?

Sample Response: I make sure the team stays motivated and engaged by giving clear instructions, communicating honestly, and being flexible at ambiguous moments.

33. Could you provide an instance when you had to collaborate with a team that was different in terms of culture?

Sample Response: By appreciating many viewpoints, actively listening, and cultivating an inclusive culture, I worked with a culturally diverse team to enhance our decision-making and results.

34. Tell me about a time when you had to handle a workplace safety issue.

Sample Response: I alerted the safety committee about a safety danger that I discovered in our office right away. I also made an effort to guarantee a safer workplace by teaching my coworkers safe procedures.

35. When you have to make choices that are controversial but necessary for the company as a whole, how do you manage the situation?

Sample Response: I make tough choices after giving them a lot of thought, taking the organization's long-term interests into account. I also communicate honestly and clearly with all parties involved, stressing the reasoning behind the choice.

36. When was the last time you had to manage a project while working remotely alone or with other members of your team?

Sample Response: By using collaboration tools, keeping frequent contact, and making sure everyone felt informed and connected, I was able to manage a project with distant team members.

37. Give an example of a crisis you had to handle that may have harmed the image of your business.

Sample Response: To preserve our company's integrity and image, I managed a PR problem by responding quickly, being open and honest with concerns, and putting a crisis communication strategy into action.

38. How do you respond to circumstances when you have to give a boss or superior feedback?

Sample Response: I provide constructive and courteous criticism, emphasizing changes and recommendations that will help the company as well as advance my career.

39. Could you provide an instance when you had to bargain for better terms with suppliers or outside partners?

Sample Response: I conducted in-depth market research, highlighted our worth as customers, and developed a long-term, mutually beneficial relationship to bargain with a vendor to achieve better prices and conditions.

40. Give an example of a time you had to oversee a project with a team that was spread out over many time zones and was remote.

Sample Response: To guarantee smooth cooperation, I oversaw a multinational project by setting up unambiguous communication procedures, scheduling meetings at convenient times for all parties involved, and using project management software.

41. How do you respond to circumstances when you have to cut expenses without sacrificing the quality of your goods or services?

Sample Response: To save costs without sacrificing quality standards, I find inefficiencies, do cost-benefit assessments, and apply simplified procedures or alternative suppliers.

42. When was the last time you had to convince someone in your company of a novel concept or inventive idea?

Sample Response: To effectively advocate for innovation and get support, I conducted pilot testing, engaged stakeholders, and presented a strong business case.

43. Give an example of a time you had to teach or mentor a less experienced team member to help them perform better.

Sample Response: I established realistic targets, gave frequent feedback, and guided a young team member. As a consequence, their performance significantly improved.

44. How do you respond when one of your teammates exhibits subpar conduct or performance?

Sample Response: I follow business standards and handle performance or behavior concerns by having private, productive conversations, laying out clear expectations, and offering help for development.

45. Could you provide an instance of dealing with a team member who often missed deadlines?

Sample Response: I had a team member who had trouble meeting deadlines. I met with them one-on-one to learn about their difficulties, extended my help, and established a deadline monitoring system, all of which had a big positive impact on their output.

46. Give an example of a time you had to manage a project with unforeseen financial restrictions.

Sample Response: To complete a project under budget, I continuously monitored spending, revised the project scope, and looked for cost-effective alternatives.

47. How do you respond to circumstances when you have to act quickly and under pressure?

Sample Response: When faced with a sudden choice, I trust my intuition, prioritize important considerations, draw on my experience, and weigh the possible outcomes.

48. When managing a project with many stakeholders that have competing interests or objectives, can you think of an instance?

Sample Response: By completing a thorough stakeholder analysis, fostering talks, and identifying points of agreement that were in line with project goals, I was able to manage a project with competing stakeholder interests.

49. Give an example of a time when you had to deal with a team member who was averse to new ideas or technology.

Sample Response: I overcame a team member's reluctance to adopt new technologies by showing them the advantages, offering training and assistance, and including them in the process of transition, all of which helped to lower resistance.

50. How do you respond to circumstances when you have to make decisions with ethics first in mind?

Sample Response: I put ethics first by comparing choices to accepted moral standards, seeking advice from superiors or colleagues when necessary, and selecting the path of action that is consistent with our moral principles.

51. Could you provide an instance of managing a project with a tight deadline that you had to work on?

Sample Response: I assembled a committed team, streamlined procedures, and worked hard to ensure project completion within the allotted period to manage a project with an exceptionally tight deadline.

52. Tell about a time you had to manage a crisis that needed to be resolved right away to avoid a worse problem.

Sample Response: I handled a crisis by putting emergency procedures into place quickly, liaising with pertinent teams, and acting decisively to stop a serious problem from arising.

53. When you have to strike a balance between opposing requests from many customers or departments, how do you manage the situation?

Sample Response: I manage conflicting demands by being open and honest in my communication, establishing reasonable expectations, and working with others to establish priorities that are advantageous to all parties.

54. Can you think of an instance when you had to inspire a team that was losing hope to accomplish a difficult task?

Sample Response: I raised the morale of a disheartened team by listening to their worries, offering encouragement and support, and establishing more manageable goals that finally resulted in the successful completion of the difficult task.

55. Give an example of a time you had to manage a project that went far over budget.

Sample Response: I oversaw a project that went over budget. To get it back under budget, I carried out a detailed cost analysis, found areas where money was being spent too much, and put remedial measures in place.

56. In what ways do you successfully manage remote teams to maintain cohesiveness and productivity?

Sample Response: To ensure productivity and cohesiveness, I oversee remote teams by doing frequent check-ins, communicating, creating a sense of community, and using collaboration technologies.

57. Could you provide an example of a project you managed that had changing objectives and priorities?

Sample Response: I oversaw a project with fluctuating priorities by remaining adaptable, making necessary revisions to the project plans, and making sure the team remained in line with the changing aims and objectives.

58. Explain a time you had to manage a project with limited staff and equipment, among other resources.

Sample Response: I oversaw a project with limited resources by allocating resources optimally, contracting out certain work, and coming up with creative solutions that helped us finish the project on schedule.

59. In what ways do you resolve issues within the team that are impeding the completion of the project?

Sample Response: To resolve team disagreements, I encourage open communication, lead conversations to pinpoint the underlying issues, and collaborate with

others to put ideas into action that bring peace
and momentum back to the project.

60. Can you think of a situation when you had
to manage a project that had to adhere to
stringent regulatory requirements?

Sample Response: I oversaw a project with
stringent regulatory requirements by working
with legal professionals, carrying out in-depth
research, and putting compliance mechanisms
in place to guarantee the project complied with
all regulations.

61. Tell about a time you had to oversee a
project with a varied group of people on the
team who had different backgrounds,
experiences, and skill sets.

Sample Response: By using each team
member's special talents, encouraging
cross-functional cooperation, and cultivating an
inclusive team culture, I was able to effectively

manage a diverse team and help the project succeed.

62. When faced with making important choices without sufficient knowledge or facts, how do you respond?

Sample Response: In circumstances where there is a lack of data, I acquire information, speak with experts, weigh the advantages and disadvantages, and, where required, lean toward taking action.

63. Could you provide an instance of managing a project where the client's needs changed frequently?

Sample Response: To guarantee customer satisfaction, I oversaw a project with changing client needs by keeping regular contact, recording modifications, and modifying the project plan as necessary.

64. Give an example of a project you managed that required you to oversee outside suppliers or contractors.

Sample Response: To ensure the success of a project involving external suppliers, I managed it by setting clear objectives, regularly monitoring their performance, and keeping lines of communication open.

65. When you have to oversee a project but have restricted access to essential tools or resources, how do you approach the situation?

Sample Response: To effectively manage such projects, I find other resources, come up with innovative solutions for resource constraints, and maximize the use of current technologies.

66. Can you think of an instance when you were required to manage a project under stringent confidentiality guidelines?

Sample Response: Throughout the project's existence, I strictly adhered to confidentiality regulations, implemented security measures, and limited access to authorized staff to manage a highly sensitive project.

67. Give an example of a project management scenario where you had to deal with ever-changing client needs or the external market environment.

Sample Response: I was able to effectively manage a project in a market that was changing by keeping an eye on industry developments, being aware of client expectations, and modifying our project plan as necessary to be competitive.

68. How do you respond to circumstances when you have to oversee a project that has to be completed quickly to seize an opportunity?

Sample Response: To optimize our capacity to act quickly and seize the opportunity, I oversee such initiatives by putting together a committed team, expediting the decision-making procedures, and guaranteeing effective communication.

69. Could you provide an instance of a project you managed that encountered major outside obstacles, such as changes in regulations or downturns in the economy?

Sample Response: To assure project compliance and success in the face of regulatory changes, I oversaw a project by doing in-depth compliance evaluations, modifying our approach, and proactively interacting with regulatory authorities.

70. Give an example of a project you managed that needed tight coordination with outside partners or stakeholders.

Sample Response: To achieve alignment and project success, I oversaw a project involving external partners by creating clear communication lines, defining shared objectives, and actively cooperating.

71. When you have to oversee a project with many stages and milestones, how do you approach the situation?

Sample Response: To guarantee that each step is successfully finished, I divide these tasks down into manageable chunks, establish clear goals, and keep a careful eye on the progress.

72. When was the last time you handled a project that needed a lot of cross-functional coordination?

Sample Response: By organizing frequent cross-functional meetings, developing a cohesive project plan, and encouraging a collaborative atmosphere, I successfully oversaw a project involving many departments.

73. Give an example of a time you had to manage a project that was essential to your company's long-term success.

Sample Response: I oversaw a project that was essential to the development of our company by putting together a committed team, obtaining the required funding, and paying close attention to every little detail to make sure the project was successful.

74. In what ways do you manage projects that require you to oversee many sites or distant offices?

Sample Response: To ensure alignment and project progress, I oversee these projects by using collaboration technologies, making sure that communication is consistent throughout locations, and traveling to distant offices as required.

75. Could you provide an example of a project you managed that needed a big budget reallocation in the middle of the project?

Sample Response: To guarantee project success, I oversaw a project that needed a budget reallocation. To do this, I carried out a thorough financial analysis, set priorities for important project components, and carefully reallocated cash.

76. Give an example of a time you had to manage a project that ran into unanticipated outside obstacles, such as supply chain interruptions or natural catastrophes.

Sample Response: I oversaw a project while facing unanticipated outside obstacles by initiating our crisis response strategy, communicating with pertinent stakeholders, and putting backup plans in place to guarantee project completion.

77. When managing a project that has to be adhered to strictly by quality standards or rules, how do you handle such situations?

Sample Response: To guarantee that projects adhere to norms and laws, I oversee them by putting in place quality control procedures, carrying out frequent audits, and working with specialists in quality assurance.

78. Can you think of a situation when you had to manage a project that was receiving a lot of media attention or public scrutiny?

Sample Response: To preserve the image of our company, I oversaw a project that was the subject of public scrutiny by forming a specialized communication team, creating a crisis communication strategy, and being open and honest in my responses to the public.

79. Tell about a time you had to manage a project with a lot of resource limitations, such as personnel and equipment shortages.

Sample Response: To guarantee project success within resource limits, I managed a project by allocating workers optimally, looking for economical alternatives, and utilizing existing equipment in novel ways.

80. When managing a project that has to be completed quickly to take advantage of a market opportunity, how do you handle these kinds of situations?

Sample Response: To guarantee a speedy turnaround and take advantage of the market potential, I handle such projects by putting together a high-performing team, optimizing procedures, and upholding clear communication.

81. Could you provide an instance of a project you managed that required you to handle sensitive data or information?

Sample Response: To protect sensitive data throughout the project, I implemented strong security measures, limited access, and followed data handling guidelines.

82. Give an example of a project you managed that needed tight coordination with governmental or regulatory organizations.

Sample Response: To guarantee project success, I oversaw a project involving government agencies. To do this, I kept open lines of communication, complied with legal requirements, and actively engaged with agency personnel.

83. When managing a project with dynamically shifting market conditions or consumer preferences, how do you respond?

Sample Response: To oversee these initiatives, I frequently gather market data, pay close attention to client input, and modify our tactics to take into account the changing needs and preferences of the market.

84. When was the last time you handled a project that needed close cooperation with offices or teams abroad?

Sample Response: To effectively manage a project with multinational teams, I established international communication channels, respected cultural differences, and encouraged teamwork.

85. Give an example of a time you had to oversee a project that significantly affected social responsibility or environmental sustainability.

Sample Response: I oversaw a project that had a big influence on sustainability. To reduce the project's environmental effects, we integrated eco-friendly techniques, carried out sustainability evaluations, and followed moral standards.

86. When managing a project with ever-changing technological needs or developments, how do you approach such situations?

Sample Response: To efficiently handle changing technology needs, I manage such projects by keeping up with technological developments, working with tech specialists, and putting agile approaches into practice.

87. Could you provide an instance of a project you managed that needed tight coordination with educational or research organizations?

Sample Response: By forming research collaborations, guaranteeing data integrity, and using research results to improve project outcomes, I oversaw a project including cooperation with research institutions.

88. Give an example of a project you managed that encountered strong internal opposition to new procedures or changes.

Sample Response: To successfully manage a project with internal opposition, I conducted change management training, aggressively addressed concerns, and highlighted the advantages of the modifications. Ultimately, this led to effective adoption.

89. How do you approach managing a project that has to adhere to rules or specifications unique to your industry?

Sample Response: To guarantee project compliance and success, I handle such projects by working with industry experts, doing thorough compliance evaluations, and adhering to stringent regulatory rules.

90. Do you have any memories of managing contractors or other outside suppliers in several locations while working on a project?

Sample Response: To guarantee project success, I oversaw a project involving suppliers in many locations. I did this by creating clear communication lines, defining contractual objectives, and regularly monitoring their performance.

91. Tell about a time you had to manage a project that needed a lot of creativity or inventive problem-solving to get past challenges.

Sample Answer: To overcome project challenges and achieve success, I used fresh ways, promoted idea production, and fostered a culture of creativity. I oversaw a project that called for creative solutions.

92. In a highly competitive industry, how do you manage projects when client expectations and preferences change over time?

Sample Response: I oversee these initiatives by carrying out continual market research, maintaining flexibility in our methodology, and proactively modifying our plans to take advantage of shifting consumer needs and competitive market dynamics.

93. Could you provide an instance of a project you managed that required you to oversee the integration of several systems or technologies?

Sample Response: I oversaw a technology integration project and made sure it was successful by working with tech specialists, doing thorough compatibility tests, and putting smooth integration techniques into practice.

94. Tell about a time you had to manage a project that needed a lot of negotiating to get to mutually beneficial agreements with customers or outside partners.

Sample Response: I oversaw a project that included negotiating with outside parties. We achieved mutually beneficial agreements by addressing concerns, holding win-win talks, and putting out value-added proposals.

95. When you have to oversee a project that has essential components outsourced to outside vendors or experts, how do you approach the situation?

Sample Response: To guarantee the effective integration of outsourced components into the project, I manage such projects by carefully choosing outsourcing partners, establishing clear expectations, and keeping frequent contact.

96. Do you have any memories of managing a project that presented major international or geopolitical obstacles?

Sample Response: By keeping up with geopolitical changes, speaking with authorities on international relations, and putting plans into place that reduced risks and guaranteed project success, I was able to manage a project that presented international obstacles.

97. Give an example of a time you had to oversee a project that called for major cost-cutting or financial restructuring.

Sample Response: I oversaw a financially restructured project by carrying out in-depth cost analysis, identifying potential areas for savings, and putting strategic plans into action that produced notable cost reductions without sacrificing project quality.

98. When you have to oversee the introduction of a new product or service into a cutthroat market, how do you approach the situation?

Sample Answer: To guarantee the product or service's effective launch and competitiveness, I oversee such initiatives by carrying out in-depth market research, creating persuasive marketing strategies, and carefully observing market dynamics.

99. Could you provide an example of a project you managed that needed a lot of communication and involvement from stakeholders to make sure the project was aligned?

Sample Response: To guarantee alignment and project success, I oversaw a project with significant stakeholder participation. To this end, I held frequent stakeholder meetings, swiftly addressed issues, and kept open lines of communication.

100. Give an example of a time you had to manage a project that significantly impacted the development and success of your company.

Sample Response: By putting together a committed team, obtaining the required funding, and putting in place a calculated plan that maximized the project's beneficial effects on our development and success, I oversaw a project that was essential to our organization's expansion.

You may show your ability to manage a variety of obstacles in the workplace and be ready for a broad range of circumstances with the aid of these situational interview questions and example replies. To stand out in the interview, personalize your answers to reflect your unique experiences and achievements.

Inquiries about the Company and Role in a Job Interview

Listed below is a collection of inquiries about the company and roles in a job interview, along with sample responses:

Concerning the company:

1. Why did you choose to work for our company?

Sample Response: Your company's innovative reputation and dedication to sustainability appealed to me since they reflect my ideals.

2. Could you elaborate on the culture of this company?

Sample Response: The collaborative and creative workplace culture encourages innovation. I like the focus placed on collaboration and the support given to fresh ideas.

3. What is your knowledge of our company's most recent accomplishments?

Sample Response: I know your business just introduced a ground-breaking product that won praise from the industry for its effect and inventiveness.

4. Who are our primary rivals, and how do we stack up?

Sample Response: [Names of competitors] are your principal rivals. Although they are really good in certain areas, your organization shines, in my opinion, because of its dedication to quality and client pleasure.

5. What are the strategic objectives and long-term vision of the company?

Sample Response: Your long-term goals of breaking into new areas and taking the lead in environmentally friendly technological solutions excite me.

6. How does this business encourage career advancement?

Sample Response: The organization provides possibilities for skill growth and constant training, which I find vital since I believe in lifelong learning.

7. What difficulties is the business now dealing with?

Sample Response: I am aware that there are obstacles to adjusting to shifting market trends, and I am eager to provide my knowledge to help solve these issues.

8. What is the company's position on inclusion and diversity?

Sample Response: I find it crucial that the organization is dedicated to diversity and inclusion, as I've read. Your efforts to promote inclusivity and your diverse staff are clear indicators of this.

9. Could you describe how the business approaches sustainability?

Sample Response: I agree with your company's commitment to environmental principles since it makes active investments in sustainable practices, such as producing eco-friendly goods and cutting carbon emissions.

10. How does the business support the local community?

Sample Response: It's great to hear about the company's charitable endeavors, which include helping out at neighborhood nonprofits and taking part in volunteer work.

Concerning the role:

11. What are the main duties involved in this position?

Sample Responses: The position entails [list important duties], such as [particular responsibilities]. It is essential to the objectives of the firm.

12. What abilities and credentials are necessary for this role?

Sample Response: Strong abilities in [mention skills] are required for the post, and key credentials include [mention qualifications].

13. What does an average day or week in this position entail?
Sample Response: Working with [name teams or coworkers], accomplishing [name objectives], and doing [name usual duties] are all part of a regular week.

14. How does this position support the company's achievements?

Sample Response: The goals of the organization are achieved by [particular contributions] that are directly impacted by this function.

15. What are the position's long- and short-term objectives?
Sample Response: I would try to [name short-term objectives] in the short term and [name long-term goals] in the long term.

16. What difficulties might this position provide for me?

Sample Response: [Name possible problems] may provide challenges, but I'm sure that [related experience] will enable me to deal with them successfully.

17. In this job, how is performance assessed?

Sample Response: To guarantee alignment with the company's objectives, performance is reviewed using [specify assessment criteria].

18. Does this job provide chances for development or advancement?

Sample Response: I agree that there is potential for improvement, and as I advance, I look forward to proving myself and assuming more responsibility.

19. How is the team organized, and who will I be working directly with?

Sample Response: You would work closely on a variety of projects with [name important colleagues] and the team, which is made up of [name team members].

20. Could you outline the current top priorities for this position?

Sample Response: Given their alignment with the company's ongoing strategies and goals, [describe priority] are considered immediate priorities.

Please feel free to modify these questions and responses to fit your unique interview situation and background.